THE SPECTACULAR SCIENCE OF
SPACE

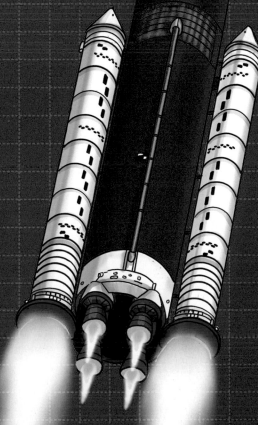

written by Rob Colson

illustrated by Moreno Chiacchiera

KINGFISHER
LONDON & NEW YORK

KINGFISHER
LONDON & NEW YORK

First published 2023 in the United States
by Kingfisher
120 Broadway, New York, NY 10271
Kingfisher is an imprint of
Macmillan Children's Books, London

ISBN 978-0-7534-7903-2

Distributed in the U.S. and Canada
by Macmillan,
120 Broadway, New York, NY 10271

Library of Congress Cataloging-in-
Publication data has been applied for.

Author: Rob Colson
Illustrator: Moreno Chiacchiera
Consultant: Penny Johnson
Designed and edited by Tall Tree Ltd

Kingfisher Books are available for special
promotions and premiums.
For details contact:
Special Markets Department, Macmillan
120 Broadway, New York, NY 10271.

For more information please visit:
www.kingfisherbooks.com

Printed in China
9 8 7 6 5 4 3 2 1
1TR/0323/WKT/RV/128MA

EU representative: 1st Floor,
The Liffey Trust Centre, 117-126 Sheriff
Street Upper, Dublin 1 D01 YC43

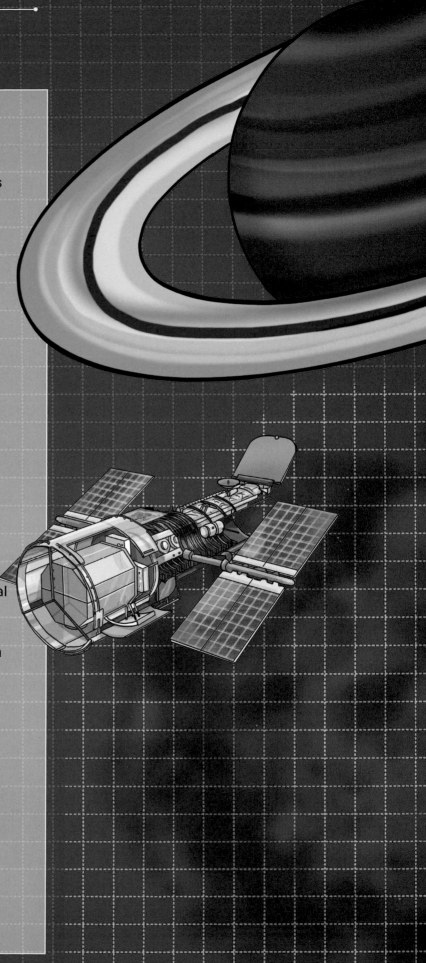

CONTENTS

OUR PLACE IN THE UNIVERSE

For thousands of years, people have gazed up at the night sky and wondered about our place in the Universe. What are the stars that twinkle at us, and why do some of them move across the sky? Over time, the secrets of the Universe have been revealed.

FLOATING IN SPACE

The ancient Greek philosopher Anaximander (c.610–c.546 BCE) was one of the first people to imagine that Earth is suspended in space rather than resting on something else. Anaximander thought of our planet as a floating cylinder with the world that we see as the flat top surface. For the first time, an astronomer was able to imagine that the Sun, Moon, and stars could pass underneath Earth as well as above it.

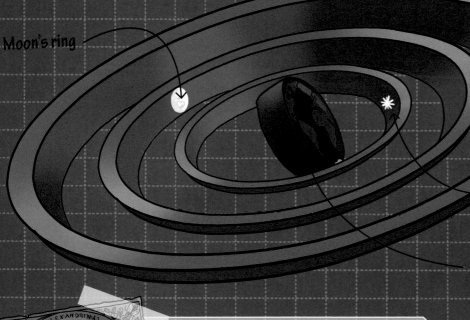

Moon's ring

Sun's ring

Stars' ring

Earth

According to Anaximander, Earth was surrounded by rings of fire. The Sun, Moon, and stars shone on us through holes in the rings.

EARTH-CENTERED

Ptolemy

Seven hundred years after Anaximander, the Greek astronomer Ptolemy (c.100–c.170 CE) made a model of the Universe that included the planets. Ptolemy placed Earth at the center, with the Sun, Moon, planets, and stars on rotating spheres. However, the planets were not always visible in the sky where the model predicted they should be. To correct this error, Ptolemy suggested that each planet also completed a smaller rotation called an epicycle. Ptolemy used his model to make accurate tables predicting where the planets would be each night.

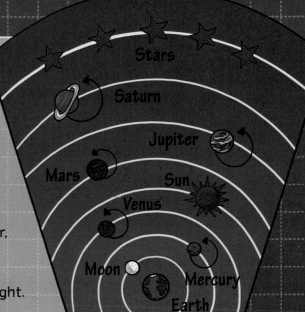

Stars

Saturn

Jupiter

Mars

Sun

Venus

Moon

Mercury

Earth

A SUN-CENTERED UNIVERSE

Ptolemy's Earth-centered model of the Universe remained the central idea until 1543. That was when Polish astronomer and mathematician Nicolaus Copernicus (1473–1543) published his idea that Earth orbits the Sun. Copernicus showed that Ptolemy's epicycles were not needed if the Sun is at the center of the system with all the planets in orbit around it. This was the birth of the idea of the Solar System.

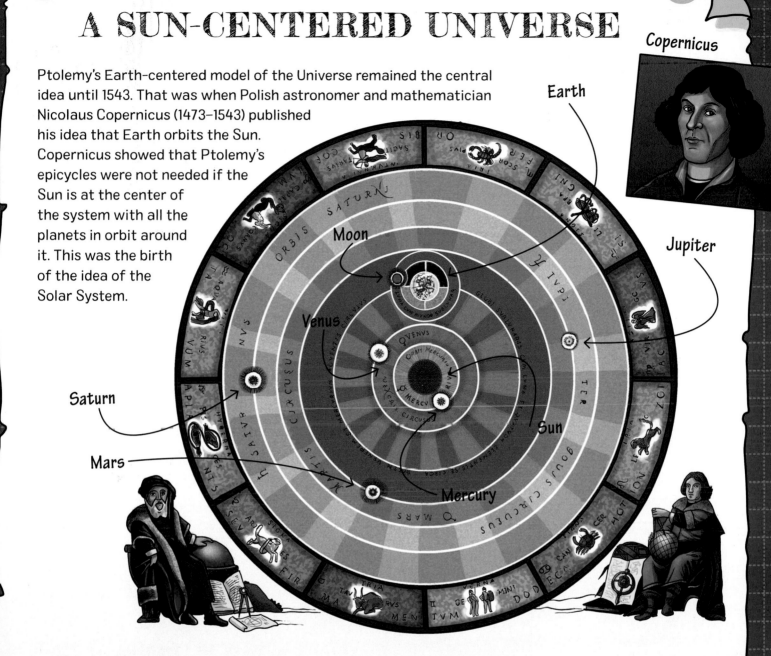

Copernicus

Earth

Jupiter

Moon

Venus

Saturn

Mars

Mercury

Sun

MEASURING DISTANCE

The Universe is far larger than ancient astronomers imagined. We measure distances in the Solar System with a unit called the astronomical unit (AU), which is the distance from Earth to the Sun: 93 million miles.

- **The furthest planet, Neptune, is 30 AU from the Sun.**

To measure the distances to the stars, we use a unit called the light year. This is the distance light travels in one year: 5.88 trillion miles. Another measurement commonly used by astronomers is the parsec. This is equal to 3.26 light years.

- **The nearest star, Alpha Centauri, is 4.2 light years from the Sun.**

THE FORCE OF GRAVITY

In 1687, English scientist Isaac Newton (1643–1727) published a new theory of gravity. According to Newton, gravity is a force of attraction between objects. It is the force that causes an apple to fall toward the ground, and it is also responsible for keeping the planets in orbit around the Sun.

Isaac Newton

ESCAPE VELOCITY

In a thought experiment, Newton imagined a cannonball being fired from the top of a very high mountain. If the initial speed of the cannonball is low, it will fall back down to Earth. At higher speeds, it will enter into orbit around Earth. At a very high speed, the cannonball will shoot off into space. The speed needed to escape Earth's gravitational pull is known as escape velocity. It is equal to 7 mi/s, or 25,000 mph.

At low speeds, the cannonball falls to Earth.

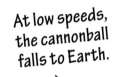

At higher speeds, the cannonball enters orbit around Earth.

At very high speeds, the cannonball flies off into space.

ELLIPTICAL ORBITS

Before Newton, German astronomer Johannes Kepler (1571–1630) showed that the planets follow elliptical (oval-shaped) orbits around the Sun rather than circular ones. Newton's new theory explained that the elliptical orbits were caused by the force of gravity acting between the Sun and the planets.

The point at which a planet is closest to the Sun is called the perihelion. For Earth, it occurs every January. At this point, the distance to the Sun is 91 million miles. The point at which a planet is furthest from the Sun is called the aphelion. For Earth, it occurs every July. At this point, the distance to the Sun is 95 million miles.

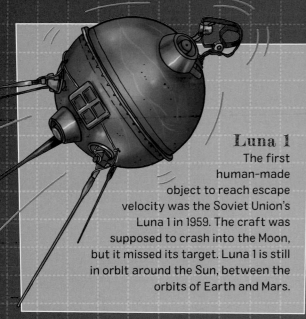

Luna 1
The first human-made object to reach escape velocity was the Soviet Union's Luna 1 in 1959. The craft was supposed to crash into the Moon, but it missed its target. Luna 1 is still in orbit around the Sun, between the orbits of Earth and Mars.

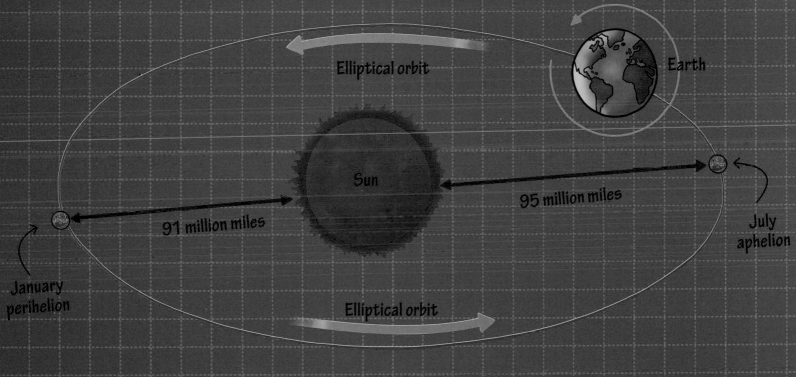

Elliptical orbit

Earth

Sun

95 million miles

91 million miles

July aphelion

January perihelion

Elliptical orbit

WHY ARE PLANETS ROUND?

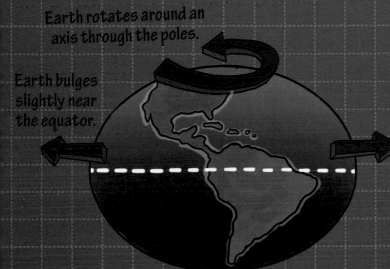

Earth rotates around an axis through the poles.

Earth bulges slightly near the equator.

The planets are roughly spherical in shape due to the force of gravity. Gravity pulls until all the surface is the same distance from the center, which means that the planet becomes a sphere. The planets are not exactly spherical, however. Because they spin on an axis, they bulge outward slightly near the equator.

THE SUN

About 1 million Earths could fit inside the Sun. It contains 99.8% of the mass of the Solar System.

At the center of the Solar System sits a burning ball of gas—a star called the Sun. Formed 4.6 billion years ago, it will continue to burn as it does now for another 5 billion years. The Sun's gravity keeps the planets in orbit around it, while its heat and light provide the energy for life on Earth.

ROTATING STAR

Like the planets, the Sun rotates on its axis. Different parts of the Sun rotate at different speeds. It rotates more quickly at its equator (once every 24 days) than at its poles (once every 30 days). The Sun's rotation was first detected by observing the way that sunspots move over time.

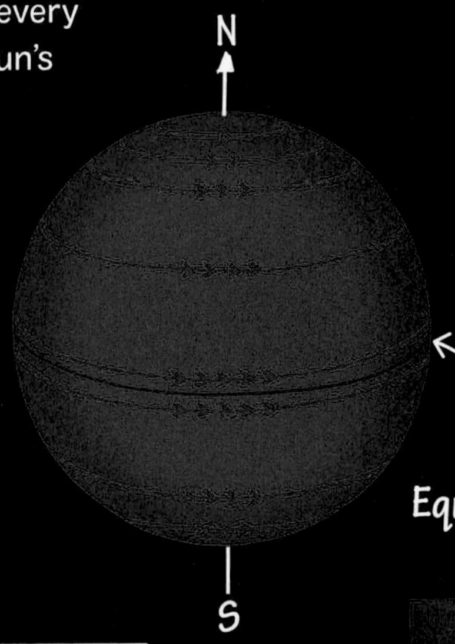

N

S

Equator

With a diameter of 870,000 miles, the Sun dwarfs the planets that orbit it.

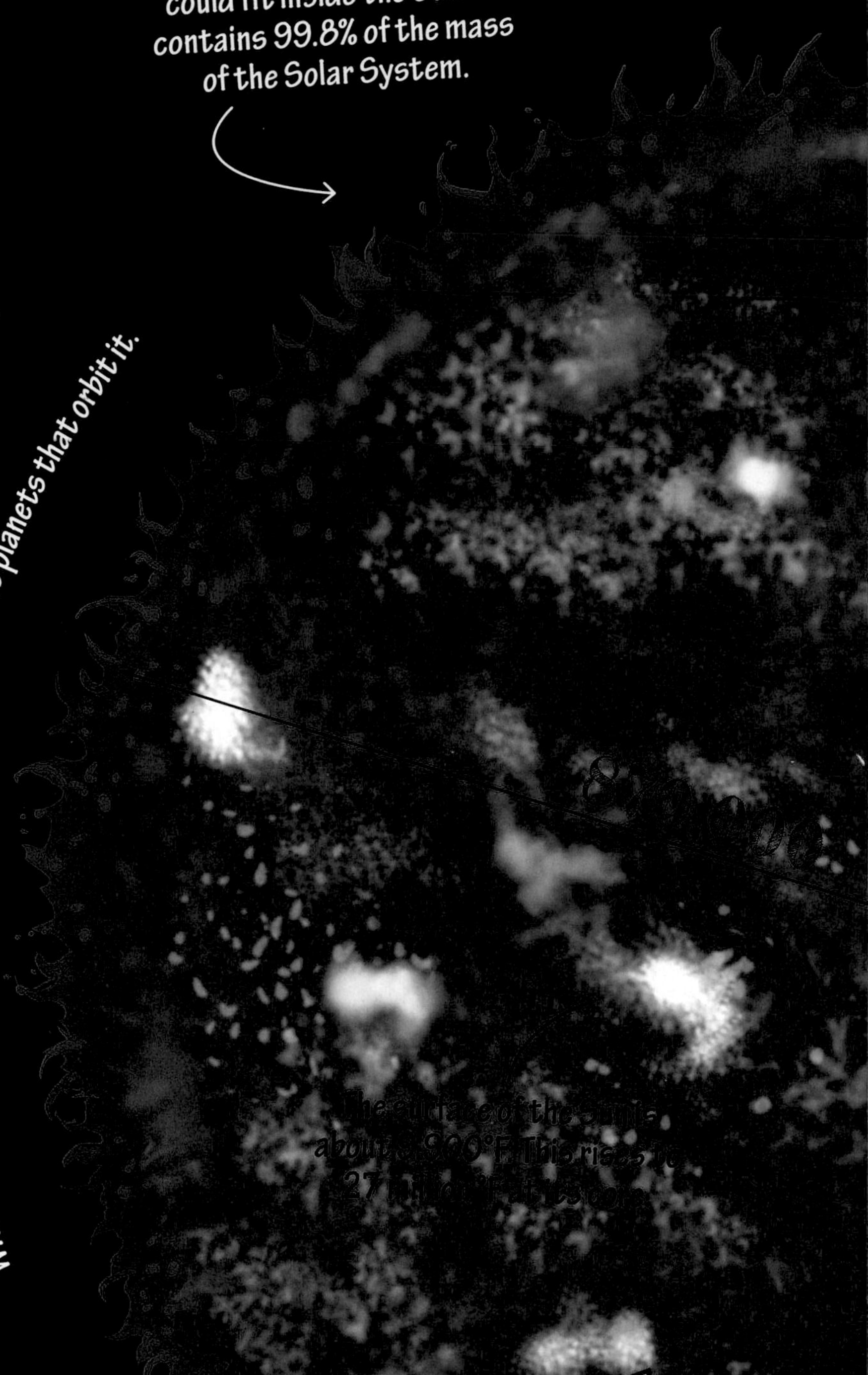

The surface of the Sun is about 9,900°F. This rises to 27 million °F at its core.

SUNSPOTS

Sunspots are areas of reduced solar activity that appear as dark spots on the Sun's surface.

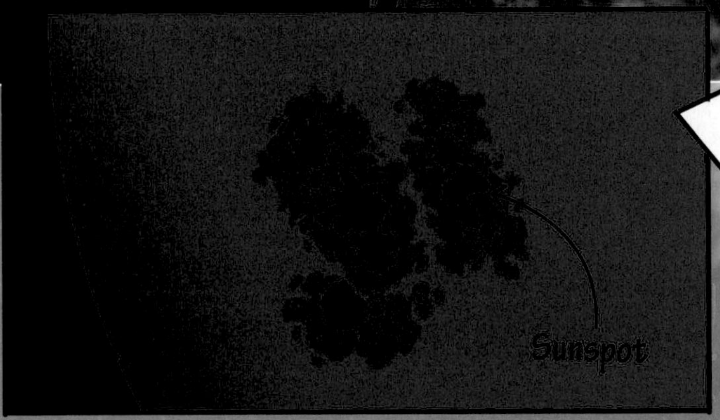

Sunspot

Solar flare

SOLAR FLARE

The Sun's surface is a mass of activity. The most active regions regularly give off intense explosions of energy known as solar flares. Solar flares may send storms of high-energy particles shooting across space. When this happens, astronauts on the International Space Station have to take shelter. Here on the ground, we are protected from the storms by Earth's atmosphere.

MAKING ENERGY

The Sun's energy comes from its core. Here, the temperature is 27 million degrees Fahrenheit, and the pressure is huge. Hydrogen atoms collide with one another and join together to form atoms of helium. This process is called nuclear fusion. About 680 million tons of hydrogen is converted into helium every second. This releases a huge amount of energy, which leaves the Sun as electromagnetic radiation.

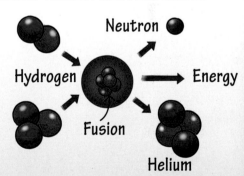

Hydrogen · Fusion · Helium · Neutron · Energy

PROBING THE CORONA

The Sun's atmosphere is called the corona. In 2021, NASA's Parker Solar Probe became the first spacecraft to enter the corona. The probe sampled the solar particles in the corona and is helping scientists to understand the origin of the solar wind—solar particles that stream out of the Sun in all directions.

Parker Solar Probe

THE PLANETS

Earth is one of eight planets that orbit the Sun. The four inner planets are small and rocky. Outside these are the two gas giants, Jupiter and Saturn. Furthest out are the ice giants Uranus and Neptune.

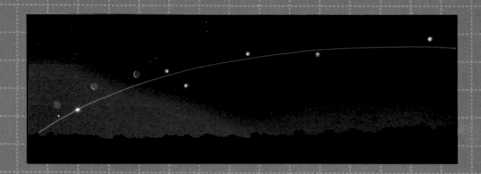

FOLLOWING THE ECLIPTIC

As seen from Earth, all of the planets track a route across the sky that follows the path of the Sun from east to west. This is because the planets all orbit the Sun along the same plane, known as the ecliptic. Our Solar System originally formed from a vast rotating cloud of gas and dust. As it span, the cloud flattened out into a rotating disk. The Sun formed in the center of the disk, while the planets formed in the outer regions.

Pluto

Neptune

Uranus

Saturn

Pluto isn't big enough to meet the third of the conditions below, so it was downgraded in 2006 to the status of a dwarf planet.

DWARF PLANET

Pluto orbits the Sun on an angle away from the ecliptic. It was discovered in 1930 by American astronomer Clyde W. Tombaugh. Pluto was classified as a planet until 2006, when astronomers changed the rules for a body to be called a planet.

1. A planet must orbit the Sun.

2. Its shape must have been made spherical by its own gravity.

3. It must be big enough for its gravity to have cleared away other objects near its orbital path.

ROCKY PLANETS

The four planets closest to the Sun are all rocky planets. When these planets formed, the temperature in the inner Solar System was more than 2,700°F. At this temperature, most of the substances within the cloud were gases. These were blown away by the solar wind, leaving only substances such as iron and silicon. Farther out in the Solar System, the temperature was much lower. Here, substances such as oxygen and methane were able to form the giant planets.

Asteroid belt

Earth

Mars

Venus

Mercury

Jupiter

EARTH'S EVIL TWIN

Venus is about the same size and mass as Earth, but conditions at the surface are very different. It is covered in clouds of sulfuric acid and the temperature reaches 890°F—hot enough to melt lead. The crushing atmospheric pressure is more than 90 times as much as Earth's.

With thick clouds, scientists are unsure if lightning can occur on Venus.

GIANT PLANETS

STORMY JUPITER

Jupiter is the largest planet in the Solar System. It is a stormy place. The Great Red Spot is a swirling vortex more than 9,300 miles wide. It has been raging for at least the last 200 years, but it has shrunk in size by two thirds in the last century. In 2019, NASA's Juno spacecraft passed over the Great Red Spot. It used microwave sensors to analyze the storm, allowing scientists to create a 3D model of it. They were amazed to discover that it extends 300 miles deep into Jupiter's clouds.

The Great Red Spot is currently about the same diameter as Earth, but it is shrinking rapidly.

Great Red Spot

RINGS OF SATURN

Saturn's rings were first observed by Galileo in 1610 (see page 28). They can be seen through a small home telescope. The rings extend out to 175,000 miles from the surface of the planet. They are made of billions of chunks of rock and ice, which are thought to be pieces of comets, asteroids, or moons that were torn apart by Saturn's gravity. Each of the rings rotates around the planet at a different speed. The inner rings rotate the most quickly, whizzing around at 50,000 mph.

Saturn's rings are on average just 30 feet thick.

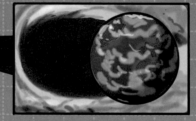

Saturn

Rings

DISCOVERING NEW PLANETS

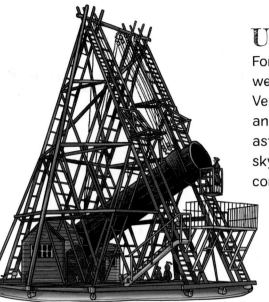

URANUS

For thousands of years, the only other planets that were known were the five that could be seen clearly by the naked eye: Mercury, Venus, Mars, Jupiter, and Saturn. Uranus had been observed by the ancient Greeks, but they mistook it for a star. In 1781, German-British astronomer William Herschel observed Uranus moving across the sky and thought that he had discovered a comet. It was later confirmed to be a planet.

William Herschel built a huge 40-foot-long telescope.

NEPTUNE

Neptune was identified in 1846 by German astronomer Johann Galle, aided by French mathematician Urbain Le Verrier. Le Verrier was trying to explain why Uranus seemed to change speed. He used Newton's law of gravity to calculate that Uranus was being pulled by the gravity of a large planet farther out from the Sun. Le Verrier sent Galle instructions about where to look for it.

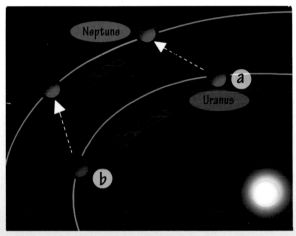

At position a), Neptune's gravity speeds up Uranus's orbit.
At position b), Neptune's gravity slows Uranus's orbit.

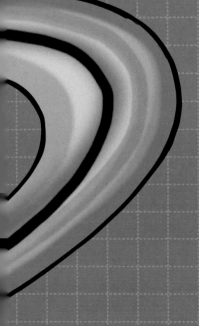

PLANET NINE

Many scientists believe that there is another large planet far beyond Neptune. Using methods similar to those of Le Verrier, astronomers have calculated that a planet about the same size as Neptune, but orbiting 20 times farther out, would explain the orbits of smaller objects in the outer Solar System. The hunt for "Planet Nine" is on.

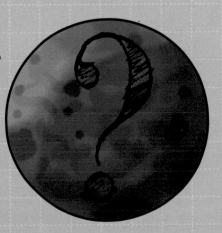

COMETS

Comets are frozen leftovers from the formation of the Solar System. There are billions of comets orbiting the Sun in the Kuiper Belt and Oort Cloud far beyond Neptune. Sometimes, a comet is knocked onto an orbit that brings it close to the Sun. As comets approach the Sun, they reflect its light and may be visible in our night sky.

Gas tail

Dust tail

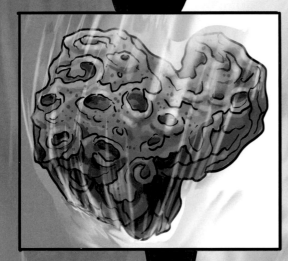

The center of a comet is called the nucleus.

DIRTY SNOWBALLS

Comets are made from a mix of ice and dust and are sometimes called "dirty snowballs." As a comet approaches the Sun, some of the ice melts and boils off the surface, carrying dust with it. This creates a glowing cloud around the comet called a coma. While most comets are only a few miles in diameter, the glowing coma can sometimes swell to the size of the Sun. Particles emitted by the Sun blow some of the coma away from the comet, and this forms a tail, which always points away from the Sun. The tail has two prongs, one made of dust and the other of gases. The tail can stretch for millions of miles.

Coma

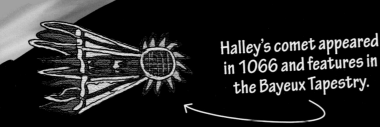

Halley's comet appeared in 1066 and features in the Bayeux Tapestry.

HALLEY'S COMET

English astronomer Edmond Halley (1656–1742) was the first person to suggest that comets orbit the Sun. Halley had studied historical reports of comets and concluded that the comets that appeared in 1531, 1607, and 1682 were all the same object. Halley correctly predicted that the comet would return in 1758. He was right, and the comet was named in his honor. Halley's comet is due to return in the year 2061.

Comet Hale-Bopp was one of the brightest comets of the 20th century. It was visible to the naked eye between 1995 and 1997. It won't be seen again for 2,300 years.

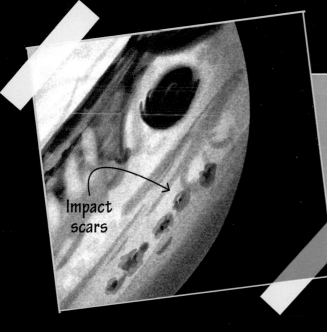

Impact scars

CRASH LANDING

In 1994, comet Shoemaker-Levy 9 crashed into Jupiter. The comet broke apart and the fragments collided with the planet over the course of several days. The collision left a series of scars in the atmosphere of Jupiter that remained visible for many months.

VISITING A COMET

In 2014, the European Space Agency's Philae craft landed on the surface of comet 67P/Churyumov–Gerasimenko. The lander bounced nearly a mile high on its initial landing. It came back down two hours later and bounced a second time before finally coming to a rest. The lander was wedged in an awkward spot and lost power after a couple of days, but not before sending back dramatic images of the comet's surface.

SPACE ROCKS

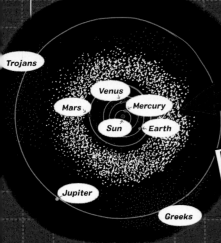

Trojans
Venus
Mars
Mercury
Sun
Earth
Jupiter
Greeks

Ceres

Asteroids are small, rocky bodies orbiting the Sun. They range in size from hundreds of miles wide to the width of small pebbles. Occasionally, asteroids are knocked off their course and hurtle into Earth.

ASTEROID BELT

Asteroids are found throughout the Solar System, but most are concentrated in the asteroid belt—a donut-shaped region of space between the orbits of Mars and Jupiter. There are about 1 million asteroids more than 0.6 mile in diameter in the asteroid belt. The largest object, Ceres, is a dwarf planet with a diameter of nearly 600 miles. Smaller groups of asteroids, known as Trojans and Greeks, share the orbit of some of the planets.

METEORS

When an asteroid enters Earth's atmosphere, it is known as a meteor. Every day, 100 tons of meteors fall into the atmosphere. Most meteors burn up before reaching the ground, leaving a bright trail that we see as a shooting star. If a meteor survives its journey to the ground, it is known as a meteorite. More than 50,000 meteorites have been found. Most are the remnants of shattered asteroids, but a few come from the Moon or Mars.

Commercial airliner maximum cruising height

Chicxulub Impactor

6 miles in diameter

Pyramid of Giza

GIANT IMPACTS

About 190 impact craters made by large meteorite strikes have been found on Earth. One of the largest is the Chicxulub Crater on the Yucatán Peninsula in Mexico. The crater was made by an asteroid known as the Chicxulub Impactor, which was more than 6 miles in diameter—taller than Mount Everest! It crashed into Earth 66 million years ago, traveling at a speed of 45,000 mph. The impact created an immense cloud of hot ash and steam, which spread across the planet and is thought to have caused forests to catch fire. The cloud blocked out the Sun for more than a decade. The dinosaurs and a host of other creatures went extinct after this impact.

The Chicxulub Impactor created a circular crater 110 miles wide.

METEOR SHOWERS

Meteor showers occur when Earth passes through a trail of debris left behind by a comet. One of the most spectacular meteor showers is the Leonid shower, which happens each November as we pass through the remnants of Comet Tempel-Tuttle. The comet has a 33-year-long orbit and each time it passes by, it creates an even more spectacular meteor storm, during which thousands of shooting stars can be seen every hour. The next Leonid storm is due to happen in 2035.

Shooting stars

Mount Everest

Asteroid watch
NASA keeps an eye on thousands of near-Earth asteroids (NEAs). If an asteroid is ever found to be heading our way, there are several ways we could stop it: blowing it up with explosives, flying a spacecraft into it to change its course, or shining lasers at it to knock it away.

THE MOON

The Moon is Earth's only natural satellite. Orbiting our planet at an average distance of 235,000 miles, the Moon is the second-brightest object in the sky after the Sun.

CLASHING PLANETS

Scientists think that the Moon was formed 4.5 billion years ago from material ejected when a planet called Theia crashed into Earth. Samples brought back by the Apollo mission (page 36–37) revealed that the Moon is made of rocks with the same chemicals as rocks on Earth. This suggests that the impact with Theia was a direct hit, causing the material of the two planets to become thoroughly mixed.

Theia is thought to have been about the size of Mars.

Sea of Showers

Sea of Tranquility

Solar eclipse

The Sun is 400 times wider than the Moon, but it is also about 400 times farther away. This means that the Moon appears to us to be almost exactly the same size as the Sun. A solar eclipse occurs when the Moon passes directly in front of the Sun, temporarily blocking out its light.

2,159 mi in diameter

Astronaut footprint

Tycho Crater

DENTED SURFACE

The Moon's surface is covered in craters caused by the impacts of asteroids and meteorites. The Moon has no atmosphere to cause erosion or volcanic activity to rearrange the surface. This means every dent in it, however small, remains there permanently. The footprints made by the astronauts on the Apollo missions more than 50 years ago are still there.

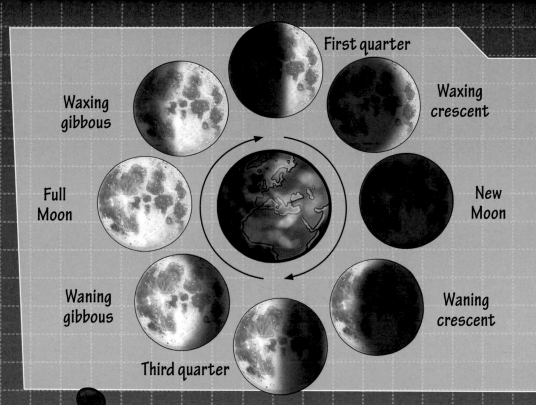

PHASES OF THE MOON

We always see the same side of the Moon. How much of this side we can see depends on how much of it is illuminated by the Sun. The Moon orbits Earth once every 27 days. As it moves, its shape appears to change as we can see different amounts of the side of the Moon that is lit by the Sun.

Waxing gibbous

First quarter

Waxing crescent

Full Moon

New Moon

Waning gibbous

Waning crescent

Third quarter

TIDAL FORCES

The oceans on Earth rise and fall twice a day in a cycle of high and low tides. The tides are caused by the gravitational pull of the Moon, with a smaller contribution from the pull of the Sun. This produces two tidal bulges on either side of the planet—one on the side facing the Moon and another on the side facing away from the Moon.

SPRING AND NEAP TIDES

When the Moon and Sun are lined up, this produces large tides called spring tides. These happen around the times of a new moon and a full moon. When the Sun is at right angles to the Moon, the tides are much smaller. These neap tides happen around the times of the first and third quarters.

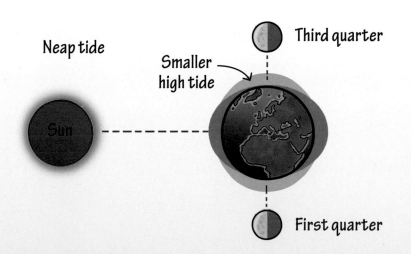

Spring tide

Large high tide

Sun

New moon

Full moon

Neap tide

Third quarter

Smaller high tide

Sun

First quarter

MAPPING THE SKY

Astronomers map the stars in the night sky through careful observation. They group the stars together to form constellations. Which constellations you can see depends on the time of year, the time of night, and your position on Earth's surface.

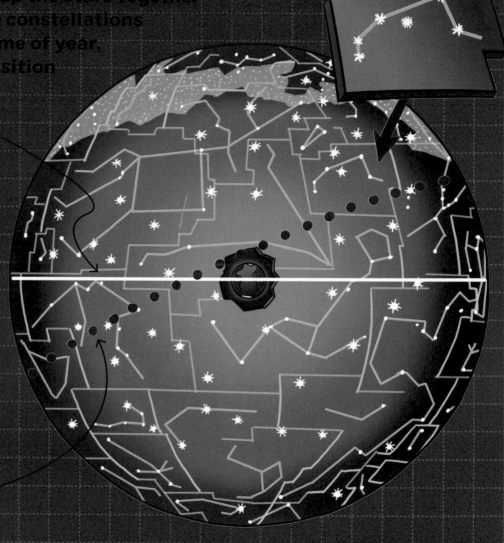

Celestial equator

CONSTELLATIONS

To map the sky, astronomers imagine that the stars are all fixed to an imaginary sphere known as the celestial sphere. They divide the celestial sphere into 88 separate regions, which fit together like the pieces of a jigsaw puzzle. These regions are the constellations. Each constellation contains prominent stars that form distinctive patterns. Many cultures have invented myths based on these patterns, imagining them to be people or animals.

The ecliptic is an imaginary line that shows the path of the Sun.

ORION THE HUNTER

Many of the constellations are difficult to see if you live in a town or a city because the street lights are too bright. Orion (right) is one of the easiest constellations to find. The Ancient Greeks imagined Orion to be a mighty hunter. Three bright stars form his belt, while other stars make up his body, arms, legs, and weapons.

Betelgeuse

Orion's belt

Rigel

NORTH STAR

Polaris, or the North Star, is almost directly above Earth's north pole. Viewed from the northern hemisphere, Polaris remains in the same place in the sky throughout the night, while all the other stars rotate counterclockwise around it. This movement is caused by Earth's daily rotation on its axis.

A time-lapse photo shows how the other stars appear to rotate around Polaris.

SOUTH STAR

Viewed from the southern hemisphere, the star Sigma Octantis sits nearly above Earth's south pole. The other stars rotate clockwise around it.

THE CELESTIAL SPHERE

Astronomers identify each point on the celestial sphere using two numbers. The azimuth is the compass direction on which the star is located. This is measured as 0° at due north and moves clockwise around a circle (360°). The altitude is a measure of the angle between the star and the horizon. 0° altitude is the horizon, and 90° altitude is directly overhead, a point called the zenith. The azimuth and altitude of a star change depending on your place on Earth and the time you are looking at it. To define fixed positions on the celestial sphere, a measure called the equatorial coordinate system is used.

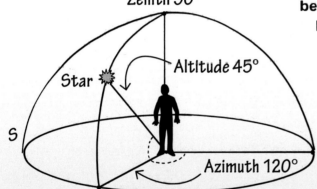

Zenith 90°

Altitude 45°

Star

S

N

Azimuth 120°

HAND MEASUREMENTS

If you hold your arm out straight in front of you, you can use your hand to estimate distances across the celestial sphere. One degree is equal to about the width of your little finger. Ten degrees is equal to about the width of your closed fist.

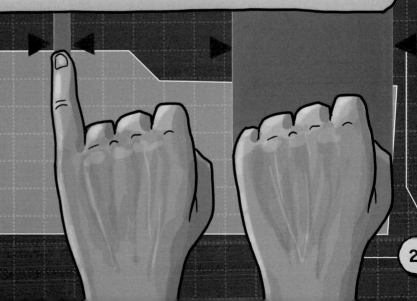

WHAT ARE STARS?

Stars like our Sun are burning balls of gas. Nuclear reactions happen at their super-hot cores, creating energy that they give off as light and heat.

Average star

Red giant

Smaller stars like our Sun use up their fuel slowly and can burn for billions of years.

The nuclear reactions continue until the star has used up most of its fuel. This period is known as the star's main sequence.

Near the end of its life, the star swells to become a red giant.

STAR FORMATION

Stars form from giant clouds of gas and dust. If a cloud becomes dense enough, it starts to collapse under the force of gravity. The center of the collapsing mass becomes a dense, hot core. When the temperature and pressure are high enough in the core, nuclear fusion begins (see page 9) and the star starts to shine. Some of the dust remains outside the star. This dust forms planets, asteroids, or comets.

Stars like our Sun gradually cool, throwing off a glowing shell of gas called a planetary nebula. The outer layers drift away, leaving a bright core called a white dwarf, which gradually fades away.

Planetary nebula

This spectacular image of a star-forming region in the Eagle Nebula is called the Pillars of Creation.

White dwarf

Massive star

Very massive stars shine brightly, but they burn through their fuel within a few hundred thousand years.

A new star

In 1604, a new star appeared that outshone every other star in the sky. At its brightest, it was even visible during the day. Called Kepler's Supernova after the German astronomer Johannes Kepler, we now know that this was a supernova explosion taking place 13,000 light years away.

Stellar nebula: star-forming region

Near the end of its life, a large star swells into a red supergiant, which explodes into a supernova that can shine more brightly than an entire galaxy. The core collapses during the explosion, leaving behind a very dense object—either a neutron star or a black hole.

Red supergiant

Kepler's Supernova has left behind a 14-light-year-wide shell of gas and dust.

Betelgeuse

The red supergiant Betelgeuse in the constellation of Orion (see page 20) is only about 10 million years old. It is expected to explode into a supernova within the next 1 million years.

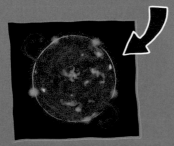

A neutron star is so dense that one teaspoon (5 ml) of its material has a mass of about 5 billion tons. That's 900 times more massive than the Great Pyramid of Giza!

Supernova

BLACK HOLES

A black hole is a superdense region of space whose gravity is so strong that everything falls into it, even light.

Neutron star

Black hole

GALAXIES

On a clear night, you can see about 6,000 stars in the night sky with the naked eye, but these are only a tiny fraction of the stars in the Universe. Stars are grouped into galaxies, which are collections of stars held together by the force of gravity. Scientists think that there are more than 100 billion galaxies in the Universe. Our galaxy, the Milky Way, contains hundreds of billions of stars.

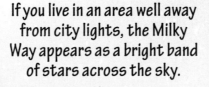

If you live in an area well away from city lights, the Milky Way appears as a bright band of stars across the sky.

TYPES OF GALAXY

Elliptical galaxies are made up of old stars. These oval-shaped galaxies contain little gas or dust and are not actively forming new stars.

Spiral galaxies, like our Milky Way, are made up of curved arms that look like a pinwheel. These galaxies contain lots of gas and dust and are actively forming new stars.

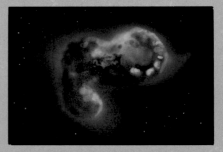

Irregular galaxies look like irregularly shaped blobs. They appeared in the early Universe before spiral or elliptical galaxies developed.

SUPERMASSIVE BLACK HOLE

In 2022, astronomers produced the first image of the huge black hole at the center of the Milky Way. Known as Sagittarius A*, it is four million times more massive than our Sun. We cannot see the black hole directly as it sucks in light, but it is revealed by a shining ring. Matter swirls as it is sucked in by the black hole, and in the process, it is heated to millions of degrees Fahrenheit and starts to glow. It is this glowing matter that we can see.

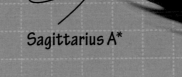

Sagittarius A*

SMUDGES IN THE SKY

In the 1770s, French astronomer Charles Messier (1730–1817) made a list of 110 smudges in the night sky, called nebulae. These are known as Messier objects and each has a number. At the time, it was believed that the Milky Way made up the whole Universe. In 1924, Edwin Hubble (see page 26) showed that Messier object M31, then called the Andromeda Nebula, was a separate galaxy. Forty Messier objects are now known to be galaxies.

The Andromeda Galaxy is moving toward us and will collide with the Milky Way in 5 billion years.

LOOKING BACK IN TIME

Due to the time it takes for light to travel across space, we are actually looking back in time when we study the skies. The Andromeda Galaxy is 2.5 million light years away, which means that we see it as it was 2.5 million years ago. The most distant galaxy yet discovered, called HD1, was first spotted in 2022. HD1 is 13.5 billion light years away, meaning that we are looking back 13.5 billion years, just 300 million years after the birth of the Universe.

AN EXPANDING UNIVERSE

Our Universe is expanding. Galaxies are whizzing away from each other at huge speeds. And not only that, but the expansion is accelerating all the time!

This artwork shows our Universe expanding out from the Big Bang. Scientists do not know how long the Universe will continue to expand.

DOPPLER EFFECT

When a police car whizzes past you, the pitch of the siren rises as it approaches and drops as it passes. This is the Doppler effect. It happens because the sound waves become shorter as the object producing them moves toward you and longer as the object moves away. The Doppler effect also occurs with light. Light waves from an object moving away become longer. This is called redshift. In 1929, Edwin Hubble (1889-1953) discovered that the light from most galaxies is redshifted, meaning that they are moving away. The farther away a galaxy is, the greater its redshift. This shows that the Universe is expanding.

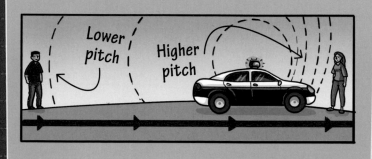

Lower pitch

Higher pitch

Edwin Hubble

Big Bang

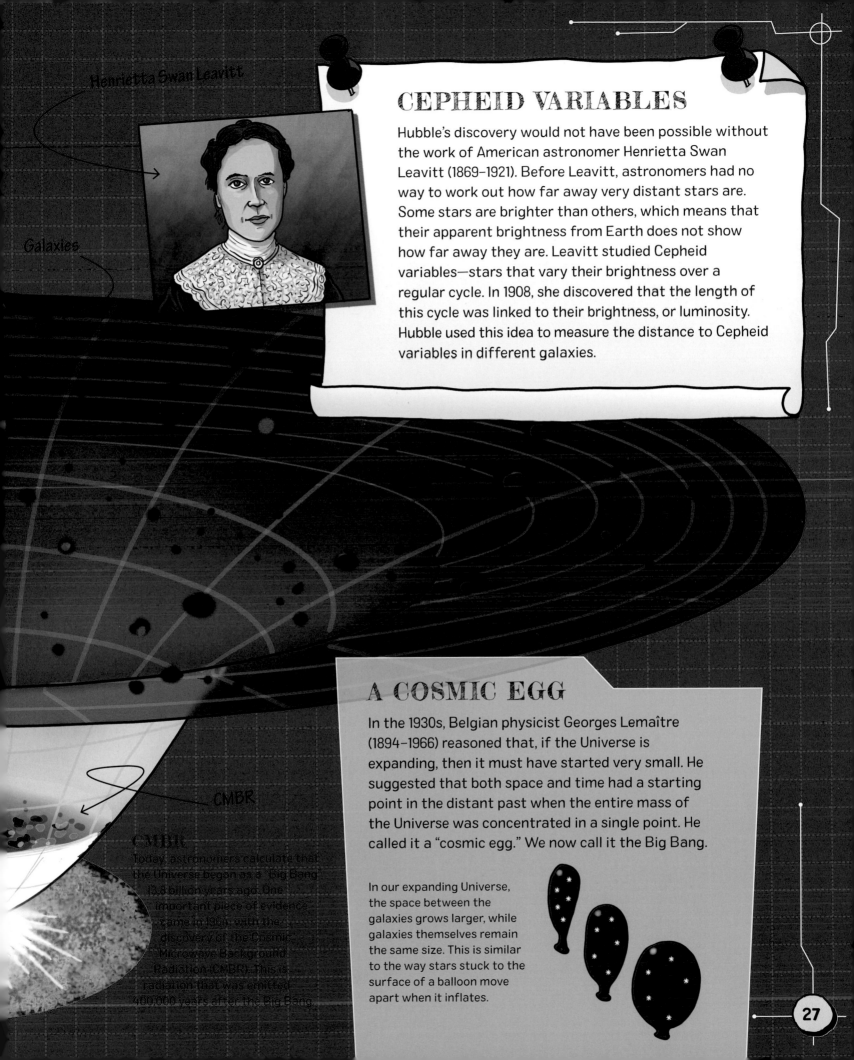

Henrietta Swan Leavitt

Galaxies

CEPHEID VARIABLES

Hubble's discovery would not have been possible without the work of American astronomer Henrietta Swan Leavitt (1869–1921). Before Leavitt, astronomers had no way to work out how far away very distant stars are. Some stars are brighter than others, which means that their apparent brightness from Earth does not show how far away they are. Leavitt studied Cepheid variables—stars that vary their brightness over a regular cycle. In 1908, she discovered that the length of this cycle was linked to their brightness, or luminosity. Hubble used this idea to measure the distance to Cepheid variables in different galaxies.

CMBR

CMBR
Today, astronomers calculate that the Universe began as a "Big Bang" 13.8 billion years ago. One important piece of evidence came in 1964, with the discovery of the Cosmic Microwave Background Radiation (CMBR). This is radiation that was emitted 400,000 years after the Big Bang.

A COSMIC EGG

In the 1930s, Belgian physicist Georges Lemaître (1894–1966) reasoned that, if the Universe is expanding, then it must have started very small. He suggested that both space and time had a starting point in the distant past when the entire mass of the Universe was concentrated in a single point. He called it a "cosmic egg." We now call it the Big Bang.

In our expanding Universe, the space between the galaxies grows larger, while galaxies themselves remain the same size. This is similar to the way stars stuck to the surface of a balloon move apart when it inflates.

TELESCOPES

The first person to point a telescope at the sky was Italian astronomer Galileo Galilei (1564–1642). In 1610, Galileo discovered the four largest moons of Jupiter, now known as the Galilean Moons. He showed that the moons were orbiting Jupiter by observing them night after night and tracking their movements. That same year, he observed the rings of Saturn, mistaking them for planets.

Galileo Galilei

Galilean telescope

The telescope used by Galileo was a refracting telescope. A refracting telescope uses two lenses to produce an image.

Convex objective lens: gathers light.

Upright image

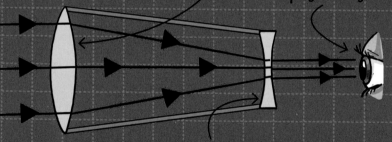

Concave eyepiece lens: turns the image into the size of your eye's pupil.

Convex objective lens: gathers light.

Keplerian telescope

Galileo's design was improved by Johannes Kepler. Kepler's design produced an upside-down image but had a much wider field of view.

Upside-down image

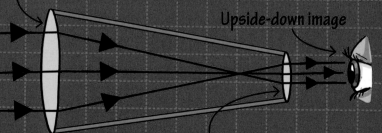

Convex eyepiece lens: magnifies the image formed by the objective lens.

REFLECTING TELESCOPE

In a refracting telescope, different colors are focused at different points by the lens, causing a blurring known as chromatic aberration. Isaac Newton fixed this problem by building a telescope with mirrors. A curved primary mirror reflects light onto a secondary mirror, which reflects the image toward the eye. Today, most large telescopes are reflecting telescopes.

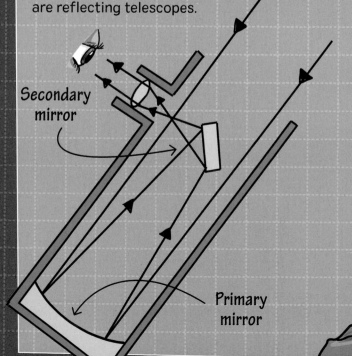

Secondary mirror

Primary mirror

RADIO TELESCOPES

Distant star

Reflector dish

Subreflector

Incoming radio waves

Signal for processing

Instead of detecting light, radio telescopes are tuned in to invisible long-wave radio waves coming from space. Radio telescopes can detect weak radio waves from very distant objects. They have huge antennas to collect as much energy as possible.

In 1967, Northern Irish astronomer Jocelyn Bell Burnell (born 1943) discovered pulsars using a radio telescope. Pulsars are rapidly rotating neutron stars that emit beams of radiation from their poles. Bell detected these beams as regular pulses of radio waves.

Radio telescope image

GIANT DISHES

The largest radio telescopes are huge structures. The dish of China's Five-hundred-meter Aperture Spherical Telescope is 500 meters (1,640 ft) in diameter.

1,640 feet in diameter

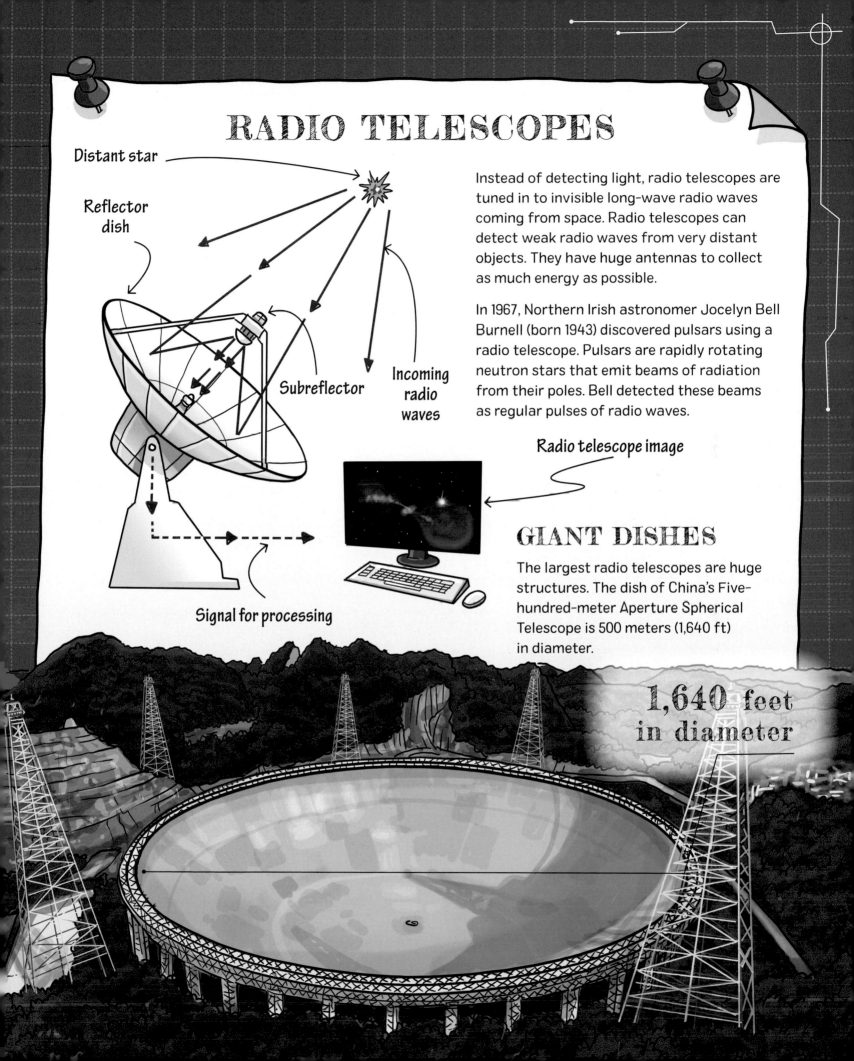

EYES IN THE SKY

Many of the telescopes on Earth, such as the Keck Observatory in Hawaii, are placed on mountain tops above most of the clouds that might block their view. However, even without clouds, Earth's atmosphere can block or distort light. The clearest images of objects in deep space come from telescopes in orbit around Earth.

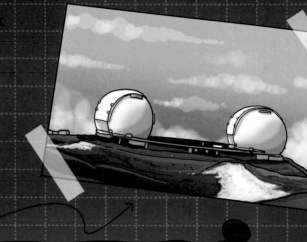

Keck Observatory

BLOCKED BY THE ATMOSPHERE

Earth's atmosphere causes two problems for telescopes. Firstly, the atmosphere distorts the light, causing stars to appear to twinkle. Astronomers call these rapid changes in a star's apparent brightness "atmospheric scintillation."

Light and radio waves are forms of electromagnetic radiation with different wavelengths. The second problem is that some wavelengths are blocked by our atmosphere. To detect these wavelengths, we need to use a space telescope.

Short wavelengths

Long wavelengths

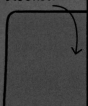

Visible light observed from Earth

Infrared light absorbed by atmospheric gases

Long-wavelength radio waves blocked

Gamma rays, X-rays, and ultraviolet light blocked by upper atmosphere

Radio waves observed from Earth

HUBBLE SPACE TELESCOPE

The Hubble Space Telescope (HST) is a reflecting telescope that has been in orbit around Earth since 1990. Since then, it has captured more than 1 million amazing images.

Aperture door

Secondary mirror

Solar panels

Primary mirror

Scientific instruments

ULTRA DEEP FIELD

The HST has allowed scientists to test their theories about the Universe. The Hubble Ultra Deep Field image has revealed galaxies formed less than half a billion years after the Big Bang. It was made by pointing the telescope at the same patch of sky for several months. Inside an area with a diameter just one tenth of the diameter of the Moon as seen from Earth, the HST discovered 10,000 galaxies. Scientists estimate that there could be 100 billion galaxies in the Universe.

NANCY ROMAN

NASA's Chief of Astronomy Nancy Roman (1925–2018) was the main driving force behind the development of the HST. In the 1970s, Roman convinced colleagues and politicians to back this ambitious project and give it funding.

JAMES WEBB SPACE TELESCOPE

Primary mirror

Secondary mirror

Launched into orbit in 2021, the James Webb Space Telescope (JWST) detects light primarily in the infrared wavelengths. These are wavelengths that are a little longer than the wavelengths of visible light. Its primary mirror is made of 18 hexagonal segments. Each segment is coated with gold. Over the next few years, it is hoped that the JWST will observe the formation of the first galaxies.

Spacecraft bus

Sun shield

SPACE ROCKETS

During the first half of the 20th century, rockets were developed that could enter space, ushering in a new era of space exploration. Rockets are devices that carry both fuel and the oxygen to burn the fuel. In this way, rockets can work in space, where there is no air.

EARLY ROCKETS

When American inventor Robert Goddard (1882–1945) proposed sending a rocket to the Moon in 1920, he wasn't taken seriously. Over the next few years, Goddard developed the first liquid-fuelled rockets and sent them as high as 1.6 miles. Sadly, he did not live long enough to see his ideas for space travel come true.

Robert Goddard

Rocket moves up

Balloon moves up

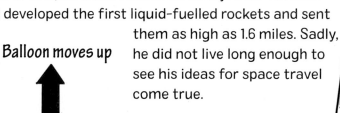

Powering through space

Many scientists did not think a rocket could work in the vacuum of space with no air to push against. Goddard demonstrated not only that rockets would work in space, but that they would work more effectively without air resistance. Fire gases at high speed out of one end of a rocket, and they will push the rocket in the opposite direction—similar to a balloon flying around the room as it deflates.

V-2 rocket

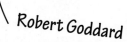

Hot gas

Air

Entering space

Goddard's rockets reached top speeds of 550 mph. This was well short of the 15,500 mph needed to enter into orbit around Earth. The first rocket to successfully enter space was a German V-2 rocket fired in 1944. It reached a height of 109 miles before falling back to Earth. The first object to successfully enter orbit around Earth was the Soviet Union's Sputnik 1 satellite in 1957 (see page 35).

THE START OF SPACE

The edge of space is normally defined as 60 miles above sea level, also known as the Kármán line. This is the point at which there is so little air that an aircraft cannot fly. Above this height, a craft must travel fast enough to enter orbit or it will fall back to Earth.

6,000 mi

Kármán line

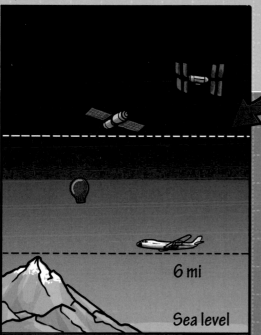

6 mi

Sea level

SATURN V

NASA's Saturn V rocket, developed in the 1960s to launch the Apollo spacecraft (see page 36), is the largest rocket ever built. It stood 360 feet tall and weighed 3,000 tons when fully fueled. Apollo was carried at the front of the rocket, which was divided into three stages.

Explosive mix
Rockets work by mixing two substances—a fuel and an oxidizer—to produce an explosive chemical reaction.

Stage 3

Apollo command and service modules (CSM)

The third stage was powered by liquid hydrogen and liquid oxygen. It took over when Saturn V was in orbit around Earth. The third stage accelerated the spacecraft to 25,000 mph—the speed needed to escape Earth orbit and reach the Moon.

Third stage

Apollo lunar module

Second stage

First stage

Stage 2

Once the first stage had separated, the second stage powered Saturn V through Earth's upper atmosphere. It burned through its fuel of liquid hydrogen and liquid oxygen in about 6 minutes, separating at a height of 115 miles.

Stage 1

Saturn V's first stage fired its engines for 168 seconds before breaking off at an altitude of 38 miles. It was fueled by a mix of kerosene and liquid oxygen.

SLS

NASA's latest rocket, the Space Launch System (SLS), is due to launch new missions to the Moon over the next decade.

THE SPACE RACE

The 1950s saw the start of a competition between the USA and the Soviet Union to explore space. Known as the Space Race, this rivalry lasted until the 1970s. Both countries invested huge resources in space exploration, leading to a series of achievements. The Soviets had most of the early successes before the Americans won the race to put a human on the Moon.

YURI GAGARIN

Yuri Gagarin (1934–1968) was launched into worldwide fame in 1961 when he became the first human in space. Trained as a fighter pilot, Gagarin demonstrated outstanding ability when he was selected as a cosmonaut, passing tests that were designed to push him to extremes. After his historic space flight, he toured the world and was greeted by cheering crowds wherever he went. Gagarin said that, "Orbiting Earth in the spaceship, I saw how beautiful our planet is."

April 12, 1961
Soviet cosmonaut Yuri Gagarin became the first human in space. On board Vostok 1, Gagarin completed a single low-Earth orbit. After re-entry, Gagarin ejected at a height of 23,000 feet and parachuted to the ground.

June 16, 1963
Soviet cosmonaut Valentina Tereshkova became the first woman in space. She completed 48 orbits over three days onboard the capsule Vostok 6.

14 July 1965
NASA's Mariner 4 completed a successful journey to Mars, taking the first close-up photographs of the planet's surface.

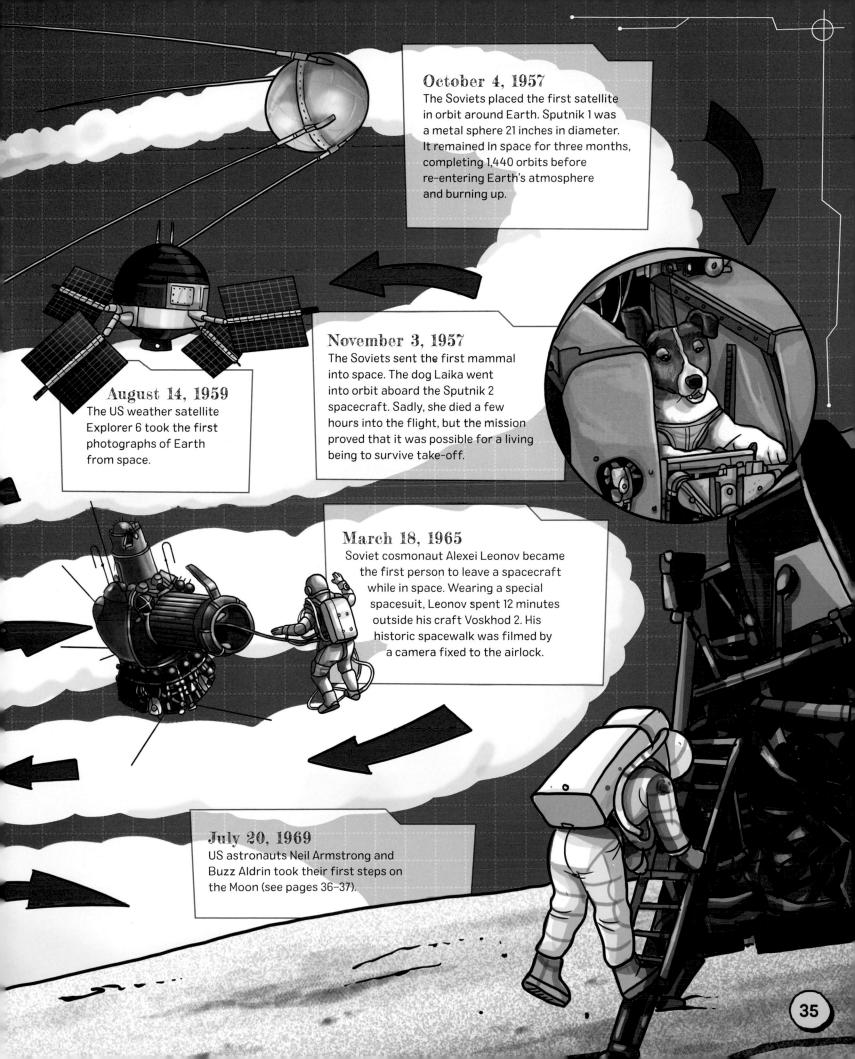

October 4, 1957
The Soviets placed the first satellite in orbit around Earth. Sputnik 1 was a metal sphere 21 inches in diameter. It remained In space for three months, completing 1,440 orbits before re-entering Earth's atmosphere and burning up.

November 3, 1957
The Soviets sent the first mammal into space. The dog Laika went into orbit aboard the Sputnik 2 spacecraft. Sadly, she died a few hours into the flight, but the mission proved that it was possible for a living being to survive take-off.

August 14, 1959
The US weather satellite Explorer 6 took the first photographs of Earth from space.

March 18, 1965
Soviet cosmonaut Alexei Leonov became the first person to leave a spacecraft while in space. Wearing a special spacesuit, Leonov spent 12 minutes outside his craft Voskhod 2. His historic spacewalk was filmed by a camera fixed to the airlock.

July 20, 1969
US astronauts Neil Armstrong and Buzz Aldrin took their first steps on the Moon (see pages 36–37).

MOON LANDING

In 1961, US President John Kennedy announced the start of the Apollo program, with a mission to put a man on the Moon before the end of the decade. Kennedy's wish came true on July 20, 1969, when astronaut Neil Armstrong emerged from Apollo 11's lunar module to set foot on the Moon.

HUGE PROJECT

Apollo 11's achievement was the result of an enormous program of scientific research and development by the US space agency NASA. At any one time, up to 400,000 people were working on the many problems that needed to be overcome.

The mission lifted off on July 16, 1969. It reached the Moon four days later.

Lunar module

The flag they left behind is still there.

HUMAN COMPUTERS

At the start of the Apollo program, the word "computer" was used to refer to people (usually women) who performed calculations by hand. One of these human computers, Katherine Johnson (1918–2020, left) helped to pioneer the use of digital computers, using them to maker her calculation of the correct trajectory for Apollo 11. The computer onboard Apollo 11 was tiny compared to modern computers, but it was revolutionary for its time as it was the first compact computer to use microchips.

SPACE SUIT

A special space suit was developed to allow the astronauts to both fly in space and walk on the Moon. The pressurised suit had many layers of protection. For the moonwalk, the suit was fitted with a backpack with oxygen to breathe, cooling water, and equipment to remove carbon dioxide. The suit had about the same mass as an adult man, but on the Moon it weighed less than a quarter of its weight on Earth. This is because the Moon's gravitational pull is much weaker than Earth's.

Pressure helmet

Life-support backpack

Protective gloves with rubber fingertips

Lunar boots

MODULES

During launch, the lunar module was packed behind the command and service modules (CSM) on top of Saturn V's rockets (see page 33). The lunar module docked with the CSM once they had disengaged from the third stage of the rocket. Together, they coasted to the Moon.

Descent
Carrying the astronauts Neil Armstrong and Buzz Aldrin, the lunar module used a rocket to slow its descent. The rocket was left behind at the landing site on the Sea of Tranquility.

Ascent
After 21.5 hours on the Moon, the ascent stage blasted off to meet the command module, piloted by Michael Collins. The ascent stage is thought to still be in orbit around the Moon.

Return journey
The three astronauts returned home in the command module. As they entered Earth's atmosphere, the outside of the module reached thousands of degrees Fahrenheit. A shield made from a special honeycomb structure protected the astronauts from the heat.

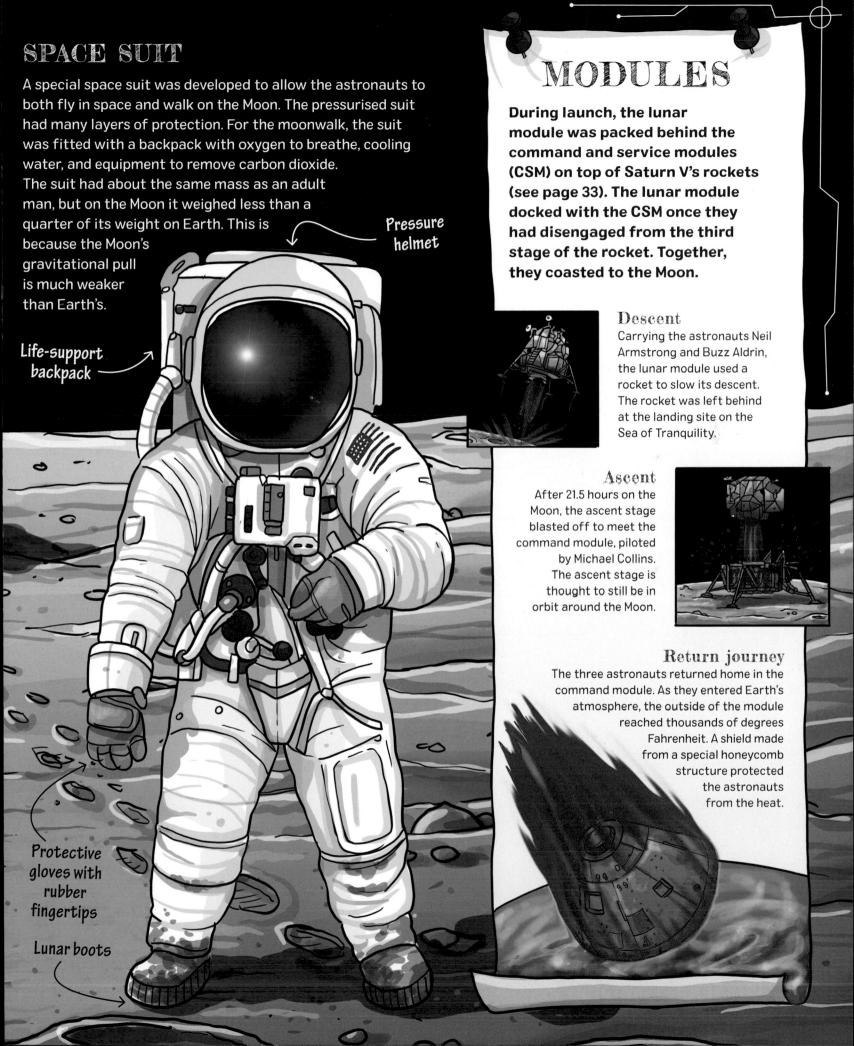

SCIENCE IN SPACE

SPOT THE ISS

To find out when the ISS will next pass over where you live, you can follow its path live on the website spotthestation.nasa.gov

The **International Space Station (ISS)** was launched into low Earth orbit in 1998, and it has been continuously occupied since 2000. Scientists from 20 different countries have carried out experiments in microgravity on board the ISS.

RAPID ORBIT

The ISS whizzes through space at 17,400 mph, completing a full orbit of Earth every 90 minutes. This means that the crew members experience 16 sunrises and 16 sunsets every day! It orbits at a height of 250 miles and is clearly visible from the ground when it passes overhead.

The ISS is powered by eight 115-foot-long wings of solar arrays.

Cooling radiator

Scientists at work

At any one time, the ISS is occupied by a crew of six astronauts. In total, more than 200 astronauts have spent time on the ISS. On board, they split their working days between scientific research and maintenance of the space station. More than 200 spacewalks have been completed to carry out repairs to the outside of the station, and nearly 3,000 scientific experiments have been performed.

Many experiments involve growing plants and microorganisms.

Repairs are carried out during spacewalks.

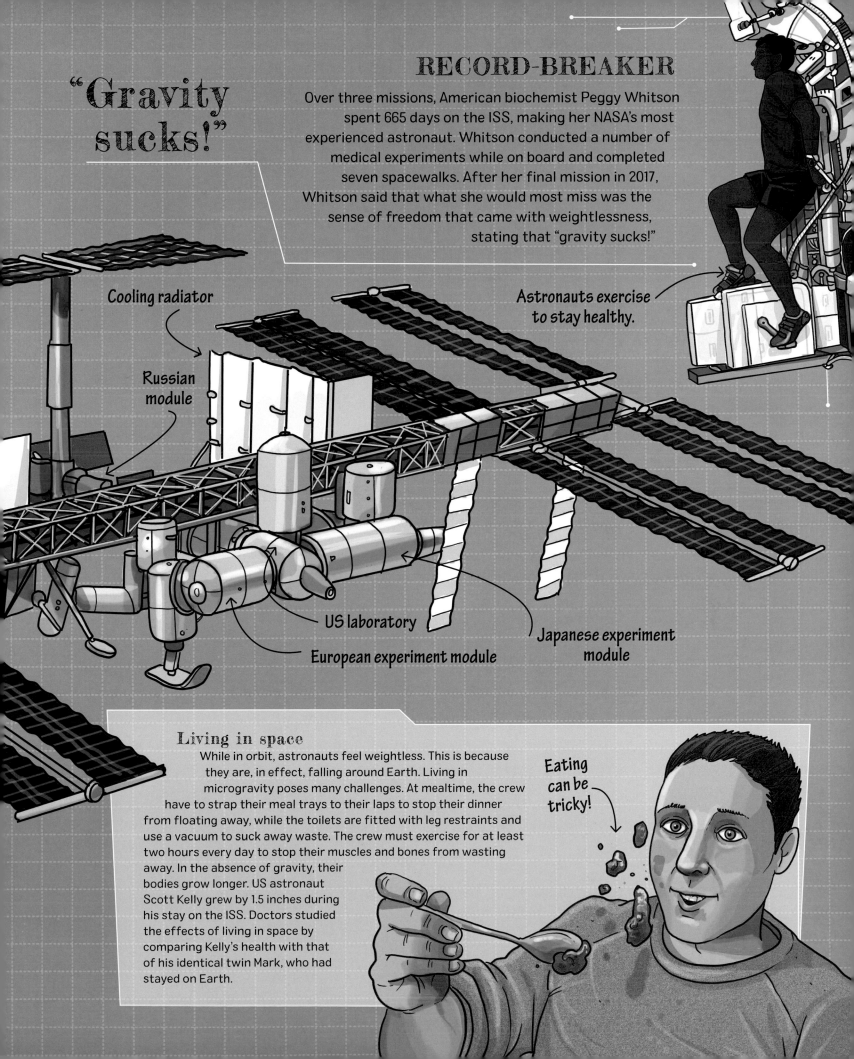

"Gravity sucks!"

RECORD-BREAKER

Over three missions, American biochemist Peggy Whitson spent 665 days on the ISS, making her NASA's most experienced astronaut. Whitson conducted a number of medical experiments while on board and completed seven spacewalks. After her final mission in 2017, Whitson said that what she would most miss was the sense of freedom that came with weightlessness, stating that "gravity sucks!"

Cooling radiator

Astronauts exercise to stay healthy.

Russian module

US laboratory

European experiment module

Japanese experiment module

Living in space

While in orbit, astronauts feel weightless. This is because they are, in effect, falling around Earth. Living in microgravity poses many challenges. At mealtime, the crew have to strap their meal trays to their laps to stop their dinner from floating away, while the toilets are fitted with leg restraints and use a vacuum to suck away waste. The crew must exercise for at least two hours every day to stop their muscles and bones from wasting away. In the absence of gravity, their bodies grow longer. US astronaut Scott Kelly grew by 1.5 inches during his stay on the ISS. Doctors studied the effects of living in space by comparing Kelly's health with that of his identical twin Mark, who had stayed on Earth.

Eating can be tricky!

PROBING SPACE

Since 1958, more than 250 robotic spacecraft have been launched to explore space. Launched in 1977, NASA's two Voyager space probes have reached farther than any other human-made object. They have now left our Solar System and are headed for other stars in the Milky Way. Between them, the probes have visited all four outer planets, discovering many new moons and capturing some amazing images.

Charged particl detector

The Voyager probes are equipped with a variety of sensors.

High-gain antenna

Magnetometer boom

Planetary radio antenna

PASSING THE PLANETS

Voyager 1 was launched on September 5, 1977. In 1979, it flew past Jupiter, sending back the clearest images of the planet ever taken at the time. The probe also studied Jupiter's moons and made the surprise discovery that the moon Io had active volcanoes. In 1981, Voyager 1 reached Saturn, flying closely past the planet's largest moon, Titan. Voyager 2 had been launched on August 20, 1977, but it took longer to reach Jupiter and Saturn than Voyager 1. This is because it was also on course to visit Uranus and Neptune. Voyager 2 reached Uranus in 1986, discovering 11 new moons and two new rings around the planet. It reached Neptune in 1989, discovering six new moons and two new rings.

1 Launch from Earth
2 Jupiter
3 Saturn
4 Uranus
5 Neptune

Sun

1

2

3

4

5

Voyager 2 route

Voyager 1 route

GRAVITY SLINGSHOT

Jupiter's gravity deflects probe's path and increases its speed.

Jupiter

The Voyager probes achieved the velocity needed to escape the Solar System with the help of Jupiter and Saturn. The gravitational pull of the two giant planets accelerated the probes as they approached, increasing their speed and changing their direction. This is known as a gravity slingshot.

Sending signals
The probes send messages to Earth using microwaves. By the time their signals reach Earth, they are very weak, and they are becoming weaker the farther the probes travel. When Voyager 2 reached Neptune in 1989, NASA had to use the combined power of radio telescopes in the US, Spain, Australia, and Japan to pick up the signal.

GALACTIC TRAVELS

In 2012, at a distance of 122 AU, or 11 billion miles, from the Sun, Voyager 1 crossed into interstellar space. This means that it has passed the point at which the Sun's solar wind can be detected. Voyager 2 entered interstellar space in 2018. Eventually, the probes will reach other stars. Voyager 2 will pass Sirius, the brightest star in the night sky, in about 300,000 years. In case the probes encounter intelligent life, they carry a record containing recordings of life on Earth.

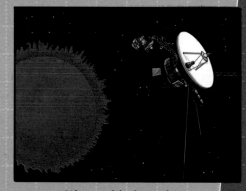

We are likely to lose contact with the probes in about 2025.

The Golden Record
Both Voyagers carry a copy of the Golden Record. It contains recordings of humans talking, music, and images of Earth. On the cover are instructions to play the record plus a diagram showing the position of the Sun in relation to 14 different pulsars. The information is written in binary code.

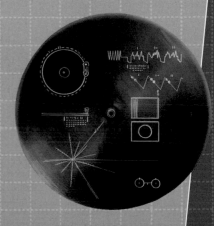

Probe approaches Jupiter from behind.

DRIVING ON MARS

Martian rovers give scientists the chance to study a larger area of the red planet than static landers. These robot vehicles have explored the surface, studying the rocks and soil. There has even been a flying rover that has taken to the Martian skies!

Balloon slows descent

Skycrane lowers rover

SKYCRANE

After using parachutes to slow their fall, the Perseverance and Curiosity rovers were lowered to the surface from a skycrane (right), which hovered over the landing site using several rockets. When the rovers were on the surface, the skycranes flew away and crash-landed a safe distance away.

BOUNCING ON MARS

On their way to the surface, the Spirit and Opportunity rovers used balloons to slow their descent before inflating huge airbags and bouncing safely on the ground. When they had come to a complete rest, the airbags deflated, allowing the rovers to roll out onto the Mars surface.

Airbags absorb impact of touchdown.

Curiosity
Curiosity landed inside Gale Crater in August 2012. Over a decade later, it was still exploring the crater, having traveled more than 17 miles. It is searching for evidence of past microbial life.

FLYING ON MARS

Powered flight on Mars is very difficult because the atmosphere is so much thinner than on Earth. The Ingenuity helicopter was fitted with two rapidly rotating blades to lift it off the Mars surface. On its first flight on April 19, 2021, it reached an altitude of 10 feet!

Ingenuity helicopter

Sojourner

The first Mars rover, Sojourner, landed on the planet in 1997. This small vehicle was equipped with three cameras. It traveled about 350 feet before it lost communication 85 days after landing.

Spirit and Opportunity

These car-sized rovers landed in 2004. Spirit lost contact in 2010, while Opportunity stayed in touch until 2018, by which time it had driven a record 28 miles. The rovers both found evidence of past wet conditions on Mars.

EQUIPMENT

Perseverance is fitted with a range of scientific equipment to carry out experiments on Mars. These include cameras that produce 3-D images of the planet, a weather station, MOXIE (an experiment to make oxygen from Mars's atmosphere), and a laser to study soil samples.

SEARCHING FOR LIFE

Are we alone in the Universe, or does life exist beyond planet Earth? The scientific quest to answer this question is known as the search for extraterrestrial life, or SETI.

TRAPPIST-1 is a red dwarf

What does life need?
Life as we know it has three main requirements: liquid water, a mix of chemical elements, and a source of energy. On Earth, the main source of energy is the Sun. Our planet orbits just the right distance from the Sun for liquid water to exist on the surface.

Water

Chemical elements

Energy

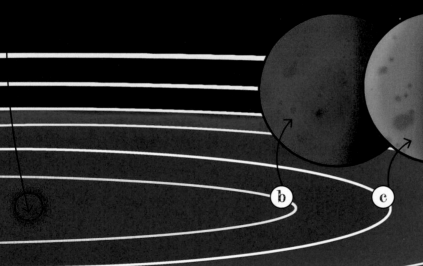

b

c

d

e

EXOPLANETS

Exoplanets are planets that orbit stars other than our Sun. The first exoplanets were discovered in 1992. Since then, more than 5,000 exoplanets have been found. Scientists think that most of the stars in our galaxy have planets orbiting around them. Some of these might have the right conditions for life. To be good candidates for life, exoplanets need to be orbiting in an area called the Goldilocks Zone—where the temperature is just for water to remain liquid.

In 2017, a planetary system around the star TRAPPIST-1 was discovered. It contains seven Earth-sized planets (labeled b–h). The middle planet, TRAPPIST-1e, is best-placed in the star's Goldilocks Zone.

Was there life on Mars?

NASA's rover Perseverance is exploring the Jezero crater on Mars, which scientists believe might have been a deep lake more than 3 billion years ago. Liquid water has disappeared from the surface of Mars (above), but the planet may once have had the right conditions for life. Perseverance will examine the rocks in the crater, looking for biosignatures — chemicals that indicate life was once present.

MISSION TO EUROPA

NASA's Europa Clipper mission is due to reach orbit around Jupiter by 2030. The spacecraft will study the moon Europa. Europa is covered in a shell of ice about 12 miles thick. Underneath, scientists believe there is a salty ocean up to 100 miles deep. Could space octopuses lurk under the ice?

f

g

h

LISTENING OUT

In 1999, the University of California started the SETI@home project, inviting anyone with a computer to help them search data from radio telescopes for radio signals from alien civilizations. Over the next 20 years, more than 5 million people connected to the project over the Internet. Together, they created the world's largest supercomputer. So far, the project has not found any alien messages, but the search continues.

The SETI@home project analyzed data from radio telescopes such as the Very Large Array in New Mexico.

GLOSSARY

Asteroid
A small rocky object orbiting the Sun.

Astronomical Unit
A unit of measurement equal to 93 million miles. This is roughly the distance from Earth to the Sun.

Big Bang
A theory in astronomy that the Universe began as a single point that expanded and stretched to create all of space.

Black hole
An extremely dense region of space whose gravitational pull is so strong that light and matter cannot escape it.

Celestial sphere
An imaginary sphere with Earth at its center on which celestial objects appear to lie.

Coma
A cloud of gases that surrounds the nucleus of a comet as it approaches the Sun.

Constellation
One of 88 areas on the celestial sphere in which a group of stars form a distinctive pattern.

Corona
The outermost part of the Sun's atmosphere.

Ecliptic
The path along the celestial sphere across which the Sun appears to move throughout the year.

Electromagnetic radiation
A form of energy that moves through space in the form of electromagnetic waves. Electromagnetic radiation includes gamma rays, X-rays, visible light, microwaves and radio waves.

Exoplanet
A planet that orbits a star other than our Sun.

Gravity
A force of attraction between objects with mass.

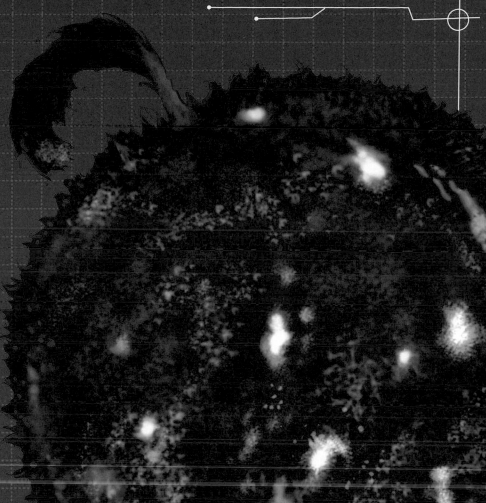

Kármán line
An imaginary line that marks the beginning of space. It is defined as a height of 60 miles above sea level.

Light year
A measure of the distance that light travels in a year. It is equal to 5.88 trillion miles.

Meteor
A trail of light in the sky produced by an asteroid when it burns up as it passes through Earth's atmosphere.

Nuclear fusion
The process by which hydrogen atoms join together to become helium atoms. Nuclear fusion inside stars releases huge amounts of energy.

Radio telescope
A telescope that detects radio waves.

Reflecting telescope
A telescope that uses a mirror to reflect an image into an eyepiece.

Refracting telescope
A telescope that collects light through a lens.

Solar flare
A sudden eruption of electromagnetic radiation from the surface of the Sun.

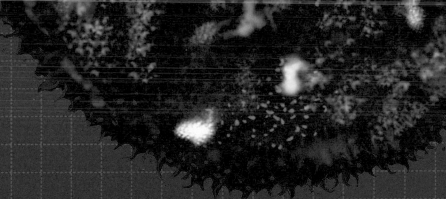

Solar System
The Sun and all the objects in orbit around it, including planets, asteroids, and comets.

Solar wind
A stream of charged particles that are given off by the Sun's corona.

Supernova
An enormous explosion that takes place when a massive star reaches the end of its life.

INDEX